4

RUBANK

SOLO AND ENSEMBLE SERIES

First Concertino

Georges Guilhaud/trans. H. Voxman

for E♭ ALTO SAXOPHONE
with piano accompaniment

First Concertino

GEORGES GUILHAUD
Transcribed by H. Voxman

First Concertino

for Eb Alto Saxophone with Piano Accompaniment

✻

Georges Guilhaud

Transcribed by H. Voxman

RUBANK®

HAL•LEONARD®
CORPORATION
7777 W. BLUEMOUND RD. P.O. BOX 13819 MILWAUKEE, WI 53213

First Concertino

Eb Alto Saxophone

GEORGES GUILHAUD
Transcribed by H. Voxman

Eb Alto Saxophone

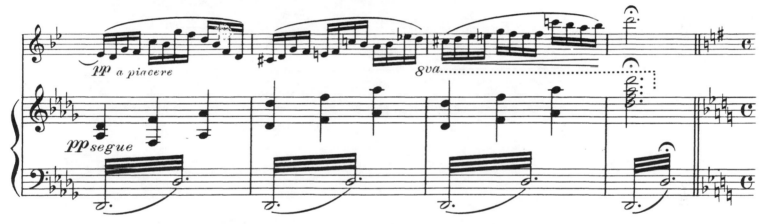

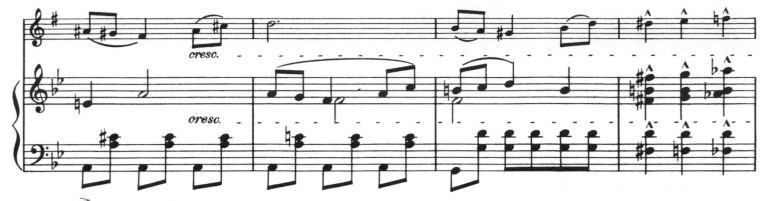

ALTO SAXOPHONE SOLOS Grade 1 to 3

with Piano Accompaniment

HL04476941	Allegretto Brillante, Op. 46 (Demersseman/arr. Voxman) *Grade 3.5*
HL04476942	Allerseelen, Op. 10 No. 8 (R. Strauss/trans. Walters) *Grade 2*
HL04479866	Amazing Grace (includes opt. duet part for alto or tenor) (arr. Walters) *Grade 1*
HL04476947	Canzonetta, Op. 6 (d'Ambrosio/arr. Hummel) *Grade 3.5*
HL04476949	Chartreuse (Colfield) *Grade 2*
HL04477490	Evening Waltz (Valse dans le soir) (Gretchaninoff/trans. Voxman) *Grade 2*
HL04477494	First Concertino (Guilhaud/trans. Voxman) *Grade 3.5*
HL04477498	Hungarian Dance No. 5 (Brahms/arr. Davis) *Grade 3*
HL04477502	Meadowland (Traditional/arr. Hurrell) *Grade 2*
HL04477504	Minuet from Haffner Music, K. 250 (Mozart/trans. Voxman) *Grade 2.5*
HL04477509	Polovtsian Dance (from *Prince Igor*) (Borodin/arr. Walters) *Grade 3*
HL04477510	Sakura, Sakura (includes opt. duet part for alto or tenor) (arr. Walters) *Grade 1.5*

SAXOPHONE ENSEMBLES Grade 3

Quartet — two alto, tenor, baritone   Sextet — three alto, two tenor, baritone

Flexible ensemble — quartet plus additional alto and tenor (opt.)

HL04479580	Allerseelen (flexible ensemble) (R. Strauss/arr. Johnson)
HL04479581	El Capéo (Paso Doble Flamenco) (flexible ensemble) (Parera/arr. Walters)
HL04479595	Finale from Quartet, Op. 9 No. 3 (quartet) (Haydn/trans. Hervig)
HL04479606	First Movement from Serenade, Op. 44 (sextet) (Dvorák/arr. Johnson)
HL04479576	Marche Militaire (flexible ensemble plus addl. alto, tenor, baritone and/or bass sax; opt. piano) (Schubert/arr. Holmes)
HL04479608	Moonrise (sextet) (Walters)
HL04479584	Pizza Party (flexible ensemble) (Walters)
HL04479599	Quartet de L'Arlésienne (quartet) (Bizet/arr. Johnson)
HL04479602	Sarabande and Air (quartet) (Handel/arr. Johnson)
HL04479604	Scherzo (quartet) (Mielenz/ed. Voxman)
HL04479587	Spiritual Contrasts (flexible ensemble) (Walters)
HL04479589	Third Movement from Symphony No. 100 ("Military") (flexible ensemble) (Haydn/arr. Johnson)
HL04477575	Three Miniatures (trio – two alto, tenor) (Ostransky)
HL04479605	War March of the Priests (from *Athalie*) (quartet) (Mendelssohn/arr. Johnson)

RUBANK®

HAL•LEONARD®

7777 W. BLUEMOUND RD. P.O. BOX 13819 MILWAUKEE, WI 53213